healing my heart

Bela H

ISBN: 9781447853169

chapters

this is the story of my first heartbreak.
to anyone going through the same thing as i did: it will get better, even if it doesn't seem like that. and you'll be thankful one day that it happened the way it happened. there is no point in overthinking it, reflecting on what you could have done better. there was nothing that could have been done to avoid it. i hope reading my story helps you get over it.

to the one who got away: thank you for everything that you taught me. you broke me, but you also made me stronger. maybe we'll have a better chance in another lifetime. or maybe i'll be the one who got away.

the beginning of a hopeless story

meeting you was so unexpected
at an unexpected time
at an unexpected place
under unexpected circumstances

i wish i knew back then
everything that i know now

maybe i would have avoided
the time
the place
the circumstances

it's funny
how you were the one
who wanted me first

and after making me want you too
you left
without notice
leaving me wanting someone
who will never want me again

sometimes i wish
i had never answered
that text message you sent at 1 a.m.
apologizing for your friends

although it was the start of our story
it was also the end of it
and maybe it would have saved me
from a horrible heartbreak

talking to you
became part of my daily routine
quickly
without realizing it

i finally had
something to look forward to
every morning
and every night

you told me you loved me
only after a few weeks of knowing me
it was 2 a.m.
i didn't know if i felt the same
because i didn't know what love was
but i just knew
that what i felt was different
from anything that i've felt before
and if i was capable of feeling love
i wanted to feel it for you
i wanted to feel it too

we didn't know what we were
for such a long time
it felt like an eternity to me
the only thing i knew was
that i wanted to be yours
and for you to be mine

i got attached way too fast
and i blame the love
that i have never gotten before for it

but we were both just two children
trying to love each other
without even knowing what love is

so i blame you too

sometimes
attachment is all we have
and it isn't so bad
after all

i still remember
the first time we met
and how my heart was racing
but when i finally kissed you
the entire world
stopped for a moment
and i finally felt at peace

that's when i knew
that you were the person
i wanted to spend the rest of my life with

healing my heart

do you remember
how you told me that friday night
that you would marry me one day?

it was our first date
and i was so in love
that i believed every word you said

falling for you was easy
it gave me warmth and security
at that time
being in your arms
was the best decision
i've ever made

 you made me look at you
in a way i've never looked
at anyone else before
i looked at you
and i saw my future
in your eyes

little did i know
that our time together
would be cut so short

i should have enjoyed it more

we were perfect
just two souls
clicking with each other
fitting like puzzle pieces
two broken hearts
healing each other
and holding onto each other

there's no one
that i trusted
the way i trusted you
with my secrets
my dreams
my fears
my insecurities
my passions

and now
i don't know
how to do that again

so many late-night calls
late-night walks
deep conversations
laughing
until we couldn't breathe
i really thought
that we were soulmates
destined to be together

healing my heart

i was stupid enough
to give everything to someone
to cross oceans
to lose myself in the process
while he wouldn't even
lift a finger for me

i wish
i could go back
to those days
when you were filling my stomach
with beautiful butterflies
when every kiss
gave me even more of them
when i felt fulfilled
and didn't pay attention
to my surroundings
you and i
was the only thing
that i had on my mind back then

i couldn't get enough of you
you were my first love
my first everything
i finally felt loved
in a way
i never did before

there was nothing
and no one
that could change my mind
about you
about us
you had my heart
trapped
for as long
as you wanted to

it wasn't long enough

your smile
was contagious
and even if you believed
the opposite
i'd die
to see that smile
one more time
i'd die
to be the reason
for that smile
one more time

you are a passionate person
so passionate
that i allegedly
turned into your passion
crazy
how passion
can be lost
with such ease

i loved everything about you
maybe too much
but how could i not love
that smile
that laughter
those eyes
that humour
that passion
how could i not love you
if you were everything
i've ever wanted

you were the best guy
i've ever met
so unique
so different
from everyone
so caring
so lovable

our story
felt like a real fairytale
for such a long time
but the chapters
were slowly
brought to a close
until we reached
the end

we shouldn't have rushed reading it

so many mornings
so many nights
so many kisses
and so many smiles
i was so certain
that you were the one
i was desperately
trying to make you
the one

we even had
our wedding song
our kids' names
our future trips
all planned
all gone
in the blink of an eye

i still remember sometimes
all the promises
that we've made to each other
how we would stay together
be there for each other
always love each other
grow old together
how this would be forever

forever is something
that shouldn't be promised
because it's impossible
to be kept by the weak

i meant it when i said forever
but you were too weak
to even think about it

i lived in fear
of losing you
in the future
maybe i should have just
enjoyed the present

and you were there
every day
until one day
you weren't

i still have
your clothes you gave me
our dating countdown
our photos together
and most importantly
i still have
all of our memories
saved inside my heart

what happened to us?

we were once
so happy together
making plans
sharing dreams
dancing in the kitchen
laughing
and talking
until 3 a.m.

now we pretend
to not even know
each other

although
we probably had
the most difficult
circumstances
someone could ever have
we were trying
to make it work
we were trying
to love each other
no matter what
we were trying

the stars aligned
but not in our favour

our love
was slowly burning away
and i was desperately
trying to extinguish the flame
trying to save us
but i found myself
being the one
who was getting burned

the heartbreak

minutes before you told me
i knew what was coming
my heart felt it
all i could say was
please
give us one more chance
we can start over

the only thing you said was
that you can't
that we should stop
that it's my fault
that you don't love me
like you used to

i've never thought
that only a few words
could break someone like that

i think the worst part
was waking up
the next morning
realising
you were gone for good

that morning
i felt for the first time
physical pain
without being hurt

and when you told me it was over
i wanted to hate you
hate you
for making me feel like this
hate you
for giving up on us
hate you
for not trying harder
hate you
for not wanting to love me

but then i understood
that hate
won't make my heart feel better
won't bring you back
and that you can't
hate the person
you love unconditionally

it is ironic
how a wednesday started our story
and another wednesday ended it

a total of 1610 days
is the time that i had you in my life
i wish it was longer
i wish it was forever

all i could ask myself that day
was *why*

why does someone leave
who once said
would stay forever?

that day
you were telling me
how love is meant to be easy
it made me feel unlovable
unworthy of love
from anyone

you couldn't have been more wrong

you told me
you didn't love me anymore
but when i looked into your eyes
all i could see was love

were your eyes lying
or did i only imagine the love
because i didn't feel it
in a long time?

truth is
whenever i looked
into those brown eyes
i saw honesty in them

so why would you say you loved me
just to break my heart
hours later
telling me
you didn't love me
after all?

i took
all the blame for it
for your lost feelings
perhaps
because you were the one
blaming me for it

i wish i knew
that in reality
it wasn't only my fault

i think that
true love starts
when you believe
the spark is gone

i wish
you'd have
thought the same

you always told me
that the only way
this is going to end
would be with me leaving you
how you were so scared
of that happening
how your heart
could never change
i believed you too much
put my trust in your words
because i knew
that i would never leave you
so how come
that in the end
you were the one doing it?

one thing
that i've always admired about you
was your resilience
and how you never gave up

but now it feels
like i wasn't enough
of a reason
for you to keep being resilient
so you just gave up
on me
on us

i wonder
if it hurt you
like it hurt me
at least a little bit

i have never thought
that i could be in love
with a selfish person

you were far away from me for years
yet i've never felt you further away
than the day you said it was over

maybe they were right all along
and long distance relationships
are destined to fail

we said that we would be the exception
that we would go against all odds
we were meant to be strong together
so where did that go?

you broke the girl
who loved you more
than she will ever
love herself

rejection
is what i felt
for months
even before you left
rejected
is how my heart felt
after pouring it out to you

i hate myself
for begging you
to give us another chance
it made the rejection
a thousand times worse

i opened my heart
in a way
i've never done before
i opened it
letting you in
believing
that you'll take care of it

what a mistake

needy
codependent
obsessive
sensitive
dramatic
i wish
i wasn't
all of that
i wish
you've never
made me feel like
all of that

it felt
like you only loved
the happy me
the sunshine me
the excited me

and when i was down
when i was unhappy
you decided
you couldn't take it anymore

suddenly
i was too much
too much to handle
too much of a burden
too much of a negative person

but maybe
i was always enough
and not seen
not heard
by the right person

my problem is
that i gave you everything
all my love
all my time
all my affection
all my heart
all of me
you had everything
and you still left
was it still not enough?

you said that
if it's not me
you don't know
who else the right one for you could be
because of our connection
our experiences together
our similarities
but then
why do you leave
the person that you think
is perfect for you?

you told me once that
if this ever ends
you will never stop loving me
you will never forget me

i wonder why you had to lie
about something like that

i've always had
a big heart
that i give
to the wrong people

when will i ever learn
from my mistakes?

i tried
everything
to make it work
while watching you
love me less
give someone else
all your attention
it hurt like hell

funny
how i have
never been jealous
only until
towards the end

it's like
my heart knew
that something
wasn't right

they say
that love isn't enough
but what if
you had everything
but no love?

i've always thought
that i was hard to love
you gave me reason
to believe it even more

i should have never allowed you
to tell me that you don't want me
more than once

healing my heart

i give
and give
and when there's nothing left
they always leave

and what does it mean
if the only person
you ever truly loved
finally leaves?

healing my heart

and here i am
months after
still missing you
and the part of me
that you took with you

healing my heart

i allowed you inside my heart
i gave it to you on a platter
you were supposed to keep it safe
not let it shatter

i hate
that now
i'll have to live
with what if's
for the rest of my life

healing my heart

you were the one
who gave me
the best memories
but also the one
who took them all
away from me
leaving me with a broken
and empty heart

78

i thought we would be walking
this hard way together
yet here i am
walking down the street
alone
with melancholy
and nostalgia
in my heart
and tears
in my eyes

you asked me once
why i was questioning
your love
but how not to question it
if i stopped feeling it
a while ago?

sometimes i wish
that i had never met you
never fallen for you
never started loving you

it would be so much easier now

healing my heart

i wonder
if you were thinking about it
for days
for weeks
for months

sleeping beside me
thinking about leaving me
telling me that you love me
knowing too well you didn't

if only
i could read your mind
your thoughts
understand your feelings
i thought i could
i thought
that i understood you
like no one else

but your mind
feels like a maze to me
a maze
without any exit
and i am lost in it
lost for a long time
lost forever
lost forever

the second time
you told me you still had
enough love
enough love to keep going
enough love to start again
enough love to fight

how can this
just change
in a matter of weeks?

why did you
come back
a second time
if all you did
was break my heart
one more time?

was once
not enough for you?

i've never felt
like a priority
in your life
it seemed like
you had time
for everyone
and everything else
i am sure
that i could have had
a ring on my finger
and still not be
the most important person
in your life
your priority

healing my heart

you used to
wipe my tears away
now
you're the one
causing them

i blame
the depth of my love
for the depth of my wound

is yours as deep as mine?

unrecognizable
your face
your actions
your attitude
unrecognizable
the way you treat me
the way you talk to me
unrecognizable
the man
i once fell in love with

it feels so weird
to come to terms
with the fact
that there's no *us* anymore
that our story
came to an end
that everything we've built
over the past four years
is suddenly shattered
in countless pieces
it feels so weird
to not have you anymore
to not have you
ever again

the hope

are we happy
in another universe?

and maybe
right person wrong time is real
and when we're ready
the universe will make sure
that it'll be the right time for us
to finally feel something
for each other again

love of my life
that's what i've always thought
that you were
that's what i've always hoped
that you were
that's what i still hope
that you are

there will always be
a spark of hope
in my eyes
hoping
that all you've been telling me that day
were just lies
and that you never stopped loving me
not even for a second

they say
that you need to let someone go
and they will come back

but i am full of fear
that if i let go
i'll never see you again

healing my heart

if we are meant to be
i'm sure the universe
will let us know
so for now
i'm letting you go
until you are ready
to come back to me

healing my heart

i can't help but read
our old messages
when we were so in love
when i was everything
you needed

i can't help but hope
that all this will come back
one day
that one day
you will be ready
you will be open
to feel it again

1500 days
that's exactly how long
our shared love lasted

but my love
will last longer

an eternity

i will always hope
that someday
we will meet again
and we will get the chance
to finish our story
that was never meant to end

and hopefully this time
we will write
a happier ending

i think what is cruel about hope is
that it somehow keeps you alive
but at the same time
it also kills you

healing my heart

you'll never feel
the lack
of my presence
the way
i feel yours

healing my heart

i wonder
if you've ever
picked up your phone
wanting to write me
and changed your mind

i'll never
understand
why people
willingly
choose to lose
a great person
with a great heart

great people
always find each other
sooner or later
at least
i want to believe that

and all of a sudden
i was stuck between
wanting to wait for you
and wanting to forget you

i didn't know which one was better
so somehow
i was doing both
at the same time

part of me will always
wait for you
crave you
wish for you
no matter how much time
has passed

i hope that
one day
we can meet again
for the first time
and finally
hold onto each other
for the rest
of our lives

maybe
it could be forever
but somehow
not yet

amnesia
let's fake it
let's forget
about the past
let's be
a new version of ourselves
and start again

i have the urge
to hold you
in my arms
to tell you
that i love
and miss you

maybe
all i need
is patience
until i'm able
to do it
again

healing my heart

i hate
knowing everything about you
knowing
your fears and dreams
knowing
all your passions
knowing
how you like your coffee
knowing
what makes you the person you are
knowing
all of your secrets

i hate knowing you
and not being able
to be with you

how is it possible
to spend so much time
without a person
without knowing anything from them
and still hope
that they'll eventually come back?

you were my home
my safe place
my best friend
my family
my person
so i believe it's normal
to hope
that i didn't lose
all of that yet

once in a while
i look up at the moon
and the stars
and remember
how we used to do it too

you were obsessed
with staring at the sky
and i was obsessed
with staring at you

sometimes
i find myself
wandering around the streets
trying to find your face
in every person
i encounter

days before
you were crying
telling me
how we used to be so perfect
for each other

i still want to believe
that we are
and that people
who are perfect for each other
always find each other

you told me
that in the future
you are confident
of being capable
of loving me
once again
but that it doesn't matter now

it made me feel
like another option
like you knew
that i am the right person
but you still don't want to love me
but what if
in the future
i don't want to be loved by you?

we were always joking
how i was
a mini version of you
so if this
doesn't work out
how do i learn
how to be
a new version
my own version
of myself?

i'd like to think
that if we never meet again
in this lifetime
that if we never look at each other again
the way we used to
that if we can never love again
like we once did
i'd like to think
that at least you won't forget me
and that maybe
we are meant to be together
but in another lifetime

we both
made mistakes
we both
messed up
we both
were supposed to fix things
maybe someday
you will realise this
and we'll fix everything
together

healing my heart

i know
that i can have
what we had
with someone else

the same love
the same happiness
the same tenderness
the same experiences

but the thing is
that i don't want
anyone else

healing my heart

maybe
we weren't ready
for each other
ready
for the intensity of love
that we tried
to give one another

life is so complex
so dealing with life
and another person's heart
is nearly impossible

maybe
we'll be ready
someday

stop
losing yourself
by still loving someone
who doesn't love you back
stop
staying with people
who don't want to stay with you
stop
seeking for his attention
hoping he will come back
stop
choosing a person
who doesn't care about you
stop
missing him
when he clearly doesn't want you
in his life

- things i've been telling myself since you left

i tried
and i tried
and i tried
when is trying ever enough?

it feels
like you are slipping
through my fingers
and i'm trying to hold you tighter
but you don't want to be held
not by me
so you are slipping away
slowly
willingly
forever

i am drowning
drowning in what if's
drowning in what once was
drowning in what could have been
drowning in empty promises
and i love you's
that we ran out of
drowning
with no one to save me
from myself
from the thought of you
from the thought of us

i've never thought
that i will miss someone
who i know
will never come back

loving you
was the best
and the worst thing
i've ever done

and i'd probably do it again
if only i could

healing my heart

they say
time heals all wounds
but my hope
keeps opening that wound
so what if it will never heal again?
how do you lose hope?

the letting go

now the heartbreak
hurts a little less every day
and i am just wondering
if i was standing right in front of you
would you have anything to say?

it took me a while to realise
that we weren't meant
to fall apart
just to fall back together
because what's meant to be
would never fall apart
in the first place

so although i held tight
onto the hope
that it wasn't the right timing
maybe in reality
i held tight
onto the wrong person
while the timing was right

sometimes i wonder if and i wish
that you're doing as bad as i am

does that make me a bad person?

how can someone
let go of the person
who made them feel something
for the first time?

closure
that's what everyone always wants

my closure was you telling me
you didn't love me anymore
while i was crying in front of you
and i think that was the worst closure
someone could ever get

letting you go
was the hardest thing
i've ever had to do
it tore me apart
and broke my heart
over and over again

but loving is the only thing
i'm good at
so i'd do it all over again

but maybe
just maybe
with a different person this time

all this time
i thought that i lost you
but i was actually losing myself
in loving you
and you were the one
losing a person
who truly loved you

healing my heart

a hard thing about letting you go
is thinking
that you don't compare to anyone

to no one in my past
to no one in my present
and most likely
to no one in my future

life is
so strange
without you
so unfamiliar
so scary
i don't want it

healing my heart

i stopped
i stopped waiting
i stopped hoping
i stopped wishing
i stopped feeling
and i started
moving forwards
towards new beginnings

i just want somebody
who's proud to have me
who wants to choose me
who wants to love me
who doesn't judge me
who accepts me
the way i am
i just want somebody
am i asking for too much?
am i too much?

healing my heart

when will i ever receive
the love i give back?

healing my heart

losing you
was really hard
but what was harder
was knowing
that you didn't want to stay

it took me some time
to realise that love
will always hurt
always be painful
and always require sacrifice
if not
it isn't love

so maybe
after all
you did love me

at least
i'd like to think that

let them go
let them see
if life is better without you

and don't look back

why would you
hold onto someone
who wants to see
if life is better without you?

once in a while
i'm sure i'll miss you

i'll miss all the songs
you've shown me
that i can never listen to again
i'll miss all the movies
that we've watched together
that i can never watch again
i'll miss all the places
we've visited
that i can never visit again
without thinking about you
i'll miss all of our inside jokes
that nobody else
will ever understand

i'm sure i'll miss you
once in a while

i can't
keep looking
for happiness
in the same place
that i lost it

temporary happiness
is what i felt
is what i'll always feel
with anyone

i think
temporary happiness
is what you were
meant to give me
when i needed it
the most

how much pain
can a person
cause you
before you finally know
how to walk away?

i forgive you
for all the pain
for everything you said
for everything you did
for everything you didn't do
for everything that's happened
and besides that
i forgive myself
for everything i did
and for not walking away
earlier

thank you for letting me go
because i would have never walked away

i heard this once
and it's true
i loved you too much
to just walk away

even if it hurt
even if i cried
even if we argued
i was willing to be yours forever
so thank you for letting me go
because i would have never walked away

healing my heart

two strangers
walking down the streets
alone
but with the best memories
in their hearts
and the most secrets
they'll ever tell anyone about

i'm sorry
for holding onto you so long
i'm sorry
for not being able to let go
of what could have been
i'm sorry
for falling in love
with the idea of who you could be
of what we could be
i'm sorry
for not seeing my worth soon enough
i'm sorry
for loving you for too long
for loving you too much
i'm sorry

healing my heart

it took me a bit
to comprehend
that you don't want me anymore
that you will never want me again
that we will probably
never cross paths again

i always said
that i could never regret you
or the time with you
yet there is nothing
that i want more
than being able to do that

this time
i am choosing myself
i can't keep choosing you
because i know
that you will never choose me back
and the only person
i know will choose me back
is me

healing my heart

there was once a version of me
before you
who was happy
fulfilled
a sunshine
so there must be a version of me
after you
who is all those things again

life has a funny way
to work things out
and i believe
that i am strong enough
brave enough
to trust life
and that everything will work out
the way it's supposed to

healing my heart

i've never imagined
that you could be
just another lesson
in my life

slowly
i am starting to forget
how you look like
your face
your eyes
your body
your voice
i miss
dreaming of you
and it scares me
because deep down
i don't want to forget
my first love

over time
i learned
to value myself
because i am worth
of so much
love
happiness
endearment

i won't let you
take that
away from me

healing my heart

i deserve
to get the love
that i give
to everyone else

i hope you know
no matter
how much pain
you've caused me
how many tears
you've made me shed
i'll never
wish you the worst

i really hope
you're happy in life
even if it's not
with me
by your side

deep down i've always known that you'd leave someday, sooner or later. i wasn't expecting it to be this soon though. our story shouldn't have ended yet, not until we had been able to write a happier ending of it. i've always hoped that we were destined to have that "forever" we've always talked about. we were so young, yet loved each other so purely. maybe we rushed, maybe we made plans too early. or maybe we just weren't meant to be.

part of me always hoped that maybe this could work in the future, under other circumstances, with more luck, because i really thought you were my person. but having no contact with you showed me that you're actually not and that i don't want you to be that anymore. the door that you said should be left open is now being closed by me. there's no point in leaving something open that has no future and is one-sided. so, this is me saying goodbye to the good times we had, to all the happiness and laughter, but also to all the tears i've shed for you. goodbye, stranger.

perhaps
we were destined
to end up as strangers

Made in the USA
Columbia, SC
30 August 2023

22276903R00100